TRUMPISMS

TRUMPISMS

THE WIT AND WISDOM OF DONALD J. TRUMP

Self-made billionaire, reality TV star, and two-time President

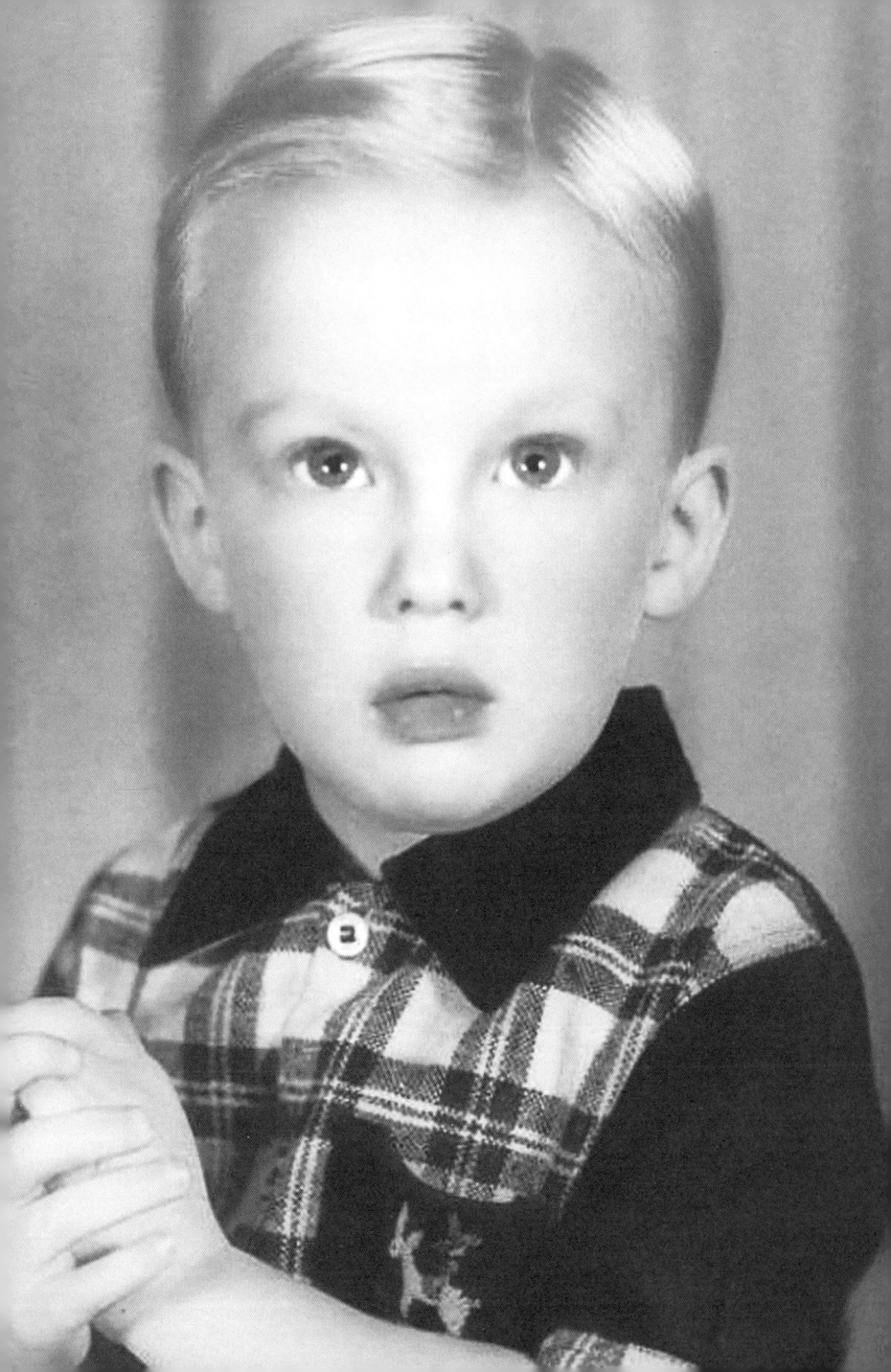

AS A BOY

"

When I look at myself in the first grade and I look at myself now, I'm basically the same. The temperament is not that different.

As told to author Michael D'Antonio in Never Enough: Donald Trump and the Pursuit of Success, *2015.*

"

"

In the second grade I actually gave a teacher a black eye – I punched my music teacher because I didn't think he knew anything about music and I almost got expelled … I'm not proud of that, but it's clear evidence that even early on I had a tendency to stand up and make my opinions known in a very forceful way. The difference now is that I use my brain instead of my fists.

Trump: The Art of the Deal, *1987.*

"

"

I always had big plans, even when I was very young.
I would build skyscrapers with my building blocks.

Trump: Think Big and Kick Ass
in Business and Life, *2009.*

"

"

I ended up using all of my blocks, and then all of his,
and when I was done, I'd created a beautiful building
… I liked it so much that I glued the whole thing
together. And that was the end of Robert's blocks.

*On his relationship with his brother Robert in
Trump:* The Art of the Deal, *1987.*

"

"

[I] always felt that I was in the military … [and had] more training militarily than a lot of the guys that go into the military.'

On his education at a military boarding school, New York Military Academy, in Never Enough: Donald Trump and the Pursuit of Success, *2015.*

"

ON HIS FAMILY

"

[Fred Trump] was a strong, strict father, a no-nonsense kind of guy, but he didn't hit me. It wasn't what he'd ever say to us, either. He ruled by demeanor, not the sword. And he never scared or intimidated me.

Playboy, March 1990.

"

TRUMP TRIVIA

Trump celebrates his 79th birthday on 14 June 2025. Other famous people born on this day include author Harriett Beecher Stowe (1811); German psychiatrist and neuropathologist Alois Alzheimer (1864); Academy Award-winning actor and singer Burl Ives (1909); TV's *Bat Masterson*'s Gene Barry (1919); former US Press secretary Pierre Salinger (1929), Polish-American writer Jerzy Kosinski; rock drummer Alan White (1949); American Olympic speed skater Eric Heiden (1958); and English pop singer Boy George (1961).

"

Part of the problem I've had with women has been in having to compare them to my incredible mother, Mary Trump. My mother is smart as hell.

Trump: The Art of the Comeback, *1997.*

"

ON MARRIAGE

"

My marriage to Marla lasted three and a half years. Sadly, like so many couples these days, we drifted apart. Our lifestyles became less and less compatible. We wanted different things.

Trump: The Art of the Comeback, *1997.*

"

"

The way I look at it, there's nothing like a good marriage. And there's nothing like having children. If you have the money, having children is great. Now I know Melania, I'm not gonna to be doing the diapers, I'm not gonna be making the food, I may never even see the kids. She'll be an unbelievable mother. I'll be a good father.

Larry King Show, *May 17, 2005.*

"

"

My marriage [to Ivana] it seemed, was the only area of my life in which I was willing to accept something less than perfection.

Trump: Surviving at the Top, *1990.*

"

"

There are basically three types of women and reactions [to prenuptial agreements]. One is the good woman who very much loves her future husband, solely for himself, but refuses to sign the agreement on principle. I fully understand this, but the man should take a pass anyway and find someone else. The other is the calculating woman who refuses to sign the prenuptial agreement because she is expecting to take advantage of the poor, unsuspecting sucker she's got in her grasp. Then there is also the woman who will openly and quickly sign a prenuptial agreement in order to make a quick hit and take the money given to her.

Trump: The Art of the Comeback, *1997.*

"

"

Well, she is terrific in bed. She wouldn't want me to say that but she is.

The Howard Stern Show, *2004*

"

TRUMP TRIVIA

Trump is of German descent, not Swedish as is often reported. Both of Trump's grandparents—Freidrich Trump (1869–1918) and Elisabeth Christ (1880–1966) were born in Germany. Trump's father Fred Trump (1905–1999) suggested that the family say they were from Sweden because of anti-German sentiment during World War II and because many of their rent-paying tenants in the Bronx were of Jewish ancestry.

Freidrich Trump (1869–1918)

"

My big mistake with Ivana was taking her out of the role of wife and allowing her to run one of my casinos in Atlantic City, then the Plaza Hotel. The problem was, work was all she wanted to talk about. When I got home at night, rather than talking about the softer subjects of life, she wanted to tell me how well the Plaza was doing, or what a great day the casino had. I really appreciated all her efforts, but it was just too much . . . I will never again give a wife responsibility within my business. Ivana worked very hard, and I appreciated the effort, but I soon began to realize that I was married to a businessperson rather than a wife.

Trump: The Art of the Comeback, *1997.*

"

"

I would never buy Ivana any decent jewels or pictures. Why give her negotiable assets?

Vanity Fair, 1990.

"

ON THE BIBLE

"

Nothing beats the Bible.

Declining to name his favorite Bible verse.
New York Times, 2015.

"

"

Two Corinthians, right? 3:17, that's the whole ballgame. Where the spirit of the Lord, right … there is liberty. Here, there is liberty … Liberty University, but it is so true. You know when I think, and that's really– is that the one? Is that the one you like?

Referring to Second Corinthians at speech at
Liberty University, January 18, 2016

"

"

Who has read *The Art of the Deal* in this room? Everybody. I always say – a deep, deep second to the Bible.

Speech at Liberty University, January 18, 2016

"

"

I'm proud to endorse and encourage you to get this Bible. We must make America pray again."

YouTube, March 27, 2024, promoting the God Bless The USA Bible, *containing the King James translation, the text of the U.S. Constitution, the Declaration of Independence, the Pledge of Allegiance and the chorus to Lee Greenwood's song.*

"

TRUMP TRIVIA

Trump's original family name was anglicized from the German 'Drumpf' (pronounced 'Droomp'). According to bustle.com, 'Drumpf' doesn't mean anything, but it's close relative 'Trumpf' is German for "trump card", a term which originated in the card game bridge but now generally referring to holding 'the upper hand' or a 'valuable resource'.

TRUMP TRIVIA

Trump's oldest sister Maryanne Trump Barry (1937–2023) was a United States District Court Judge for the District of New Jersey. In 1999, she was nominated for the position of Federal appeals court judge by then President Bill Clinton and was unanimously confirmed by the US Senate.

ON WOMEN

"

I love women. They've come into my life. They've gone out of my life. Even those who have exited somewhat ungracefully still have a place in my heart.

Trump: The Art of the Comeback, *1997.*

"

"

All of the women on *The Apprentice* flirted with me – consciously or unconsciously. That's to be expected.

Trump: How to Get Rich, *with Meredith McIver, 2004.*

"

> You know, it really doesn't matter what [the media] write as long as you've got a young and beautiful piece of ass.

Quoted in Esquire *magazine, 1991.*

> I think the only difference between me and the other candidates is that I'm more honest and my women are beautiful.

New York Times, *November 1999.*

> I've said if Ivanka weren't my daughter, perhaps I'd be dating her.

Appearing on ABC's The View *with daughter to promote* The Apprentice, *2006.*

"

Well, Rosie O'Donnell's disgusting, both inside and out. You take a look at her, she's a slob. She talks like a truck driver … If I were running *The View*, I'd fire Rosie O'Donnell. I mean, I'd look at her right in that fat, ugly face of hers, I'd say 'Rosie, you're fired.

Entertainment Tonight, December 12, 2006.

"

"

I have a daughter named Ivanka and a wife named Melania who constantly want me to talk about women's health issues because they know how I feel about it and they know how I feel about women. I respect women, I love women, I cherish women.

Speaking in Manchester New Hampshire at the Problem Solvers Convention, October 12, 2015.

"

"

I only have one regret in the women department – that I never had the opportunity to court Lady Diana Spencer. I met her on a number of occasions … She was a genuine princess – a dream lady.

Trump: The Art of the Comeback, 1997. Trump later told The Howard Stern Show in 2000 that he would have slept with her "without hesitation" … she had the height, she had the beauty, she had the skin … she was crazy, but these are minor details."

"

"

Cher is somewhat of a loser. She's lonely. She's unhappy. She's very miserable. And her sound-enhanced and computer-enhanced music doesn't do it for me … I've watched her over the years. I knew her a little bit. And you know, she reminds me of Rosie [O'Donnell] with slightly more talent, not much more talent, but slightly more talent.

In a May 2012 interview with Fox News' *Greta Van Susteren.*

"

"

If I told the real stories of my experiences with women, often seemingly very happily married and important women, this book would be a guaranteed bestseller.

Trump: The Art of the Comeback, *1997.*

"

"

Everyone knows I am right that Robert Pattinson should dump Kristen Stewart. In a couple of years, he will thank me. Be smart, Robert.

Twitter, October 23, 2012

"

"

Arianna Huffington is unattractive both inside and out. I fully understand why her former husband left her for a man – he made a good decision.

Twitter, August 28, 2012.

"

> Heidi Klum. Sadly, she's no longer a 10.
>
> *In an August 2015 interview with the* New York Times. *Klum, aged 42, later posted a video on Twitter in which a man wearing a Donald Trump mask ripped a number 10 off her t-shirt to reveal a 9.99 sign underneath.*

> Women have one of the great acts of all time. The smart ones act very feminine and needy, but inside they are real killers. The person who came up with the expression 'the weaker sex' was either very naïve or had to be kidding. I have seen women manipulate men with just a twitch of their eye – or perhaps another body part.
>
> Trump: The Art of the Comeback, *1997.*

"

Look at that face! Would anyone vote for that?
Can you imagine that, the face of our next president?'

*Donald Trump on rival Carly Fiorina, September 9,
2015 with* Rolling Stone. *He later backtracked during
the GOP debate saying 'I think she's got a beautiful face.
And I think she's a beautiful woman.'*

"

"

'I don't have a lot of respect for Megyn Kelly, she came
out, reading her little script, trying to be tough and sharp.
I got out there they start saying all this stuff … she gets out
and she starts asking me all sorts of ridiculous questions.
You could see there was blood coming out of her eyes,
blood coming out of her wherever … you could see
she was off-base. She's a lightweight.

August 2015 CNN interview, shortly after the Fox
News *GOP debate, when he denied his comments were a
reference to Kelly's personal hygiene, August 7, 2015. In
2024 Megyn Kelly supported Trump in his return to the
prresidency.*

"

TRUMP TRIVIA

Trump's mother Mary Ann MacLeod was born in Scotland in 1912. Mary met Donald Trump's father, Fred, during a family vacation in New York in the 1930s. She died in 2000.

TRUMP TRIVIA

Trump is the fourth of five children born to Fred and Mary Trump: Maryanne (born 1937), a federal appeals court judge; Frederick 'Fred' Jr. (1938–81); Elizabeth (born 1942), an executive assistant at Chase Manhattan Bank; Donald (born 1946); and Robert (born 1948), president of his father's property management company.

"

I've never had any trouble in bed, but if I'd had affairs with half the starlets and female athletes the newspapers linked me with, I'd have no time to breathe.

Trump: Surviving at the Top, *1990.*

"

"

While @BetteMidler is an extremely unattractive woman, I refuse to say that because I always insist on being politically correct.

Twitter post, October 29, 2012

"

"

". @cher--I don't wear a "rug" – it's mine. And I promise not to talk about your massive plastic surgeries that didn't work."

Twitter post regarding Cher, November 14, 2012

"

> I better use some Tic Tacs just in case I start kissing her. You know I'm automatically attracted to beautiful — I just start kissing them. It's like a magnet. Just kiss. I don't even wait. And when you're a star, they let you do it. You can do anything. Grab 'em by the pussy. You can do anything.

Hot mike captures Trump talking to Billy Bush September 2005 in the NBC Studios parking lot

> STATEMENT FROM DONALD J. TRUMP
> This was locker room banter, a private conversation that took place many years ago. Bill Clinton has said far worse to me on the golf course— not even close. I apologize if anyone was offended.

Statement on the Trump–Pence Make America Great Again! website, after the hot-mike quote became public, October 7, 2016

ON PRO-LIFE OR PRO-CHOICE

"

There has to be some form of punishment.

After MSNBC's Chris Matthews asks Trump 'Do you believe in punishment for abortion, yes or no, as a principle?', March 29, 2016.

"

"

That was a hypothetical question.
That was not a wrong answer.

Trump backtracks about his answer to Fox News *host Sean Hannity, April 4, 2016.*

"

"

I am pro-life [and] against gun control.

Addressing the Conservative Political Action Conference, February 10, 2011.

"

ON BUSINESS

"

I had loftier dreams and visions. And there was no way to implement them building houses in the boroughs.

Trump: The Art of the Deal, *1987.*

"

"

When I build something for somebody, I always add $50 million or $60 million onto the price. My guys come in, they say it's going to cost $75 million. I say it's going to cost $125 million, and I build it for $100 million. Basically, I did a lousy job. But they think I did a great job.

The Candidate, *2007.*

"

"

I try to pay as little tax as possible … It's a little tax.

In response to requests that Trump release his tax returns. This Week, ABC Network, 2016.

"

"

I do play with the bankruptcy laws –
they're very good for me.

*On the declarations of bankruptcy made on
Trump's hotel and casino. Newsweek, 2011.*

"

"

When somebody tries to sucker-punch me, when
they're after my ass, I push back a hell of a lot harder
than I was pushed in the first place. If somebody tries
to push me around, he's going to pay a price. Those
people don't come back for seconds. I don't like being
pushed around or taken advantage of.

Playboy, *March 1990.*

"

"

I don't think it's a failure, it's a success … In this case, it was just something that worked better than other alternatives. It's really just a technical thing, but it came together.

On the bankruptcy of Trump's casino empire in 2004, which allowed him to renegotiate the billion dollar debt. The Early Show, *CBS Marketwatch, 2004.*

"

"

When these people walk in the room, they don't say, "Oh, hello! How's the weather? It's so beautiful outside. Isn't it lovely? How are the Yankees doing? Oh, they're doing wonderful. Great." [Asians] say, "We want deal!"

Discussing Asians at a rally in Iowa, 2015.

"

TRUMP TRIVIA

Trump attended elementary and junior high school in Queens, N.Y., but after getting into trouble for his ill-discipline, his parents moved him to the New York Military Academy.

TRUMP TRIVIA

In 2006, Trump bought a huge estate in Scotland and built a luxury golf course on the property. According the the 2011 documentary *You've been Trumped,* after promising the local community that its construction would produce 6,000 jobs, it produced just 200.

"

I have made the tough decisions, always with an eye toward the bottom line. Perhaps it's time America was run like a business.

The Advocate, *2000.*

"

"

I study people and in every negotiation, I weigh how tough I should appear. I can be a killer and a nice guy. You have to be everything. You have to be strong. You have to be sweet. You have to be ruthless. And I don't think any of it can be learned. Either you have it or you don't. And that is why most kids can get straight As in school but fail in life.

Playboy, *March 1990.*

"

ON AIDS

"

I've been so lucky in terms of that whole world. It is a dangerous world out there. It's scary, like Vietnam. Sort of like the Vietnam-era. It is my personal Vietnam. I feel like a great and very brave soldier.

From an interview with shock jock, Howard Stern in 1997, in response to his early dating life in which he described himself as 'lucky' to have avoided AIDS and other sexually-transmitted diseases..

"

ON AFRO-AMERICANS

"

A well-educated black has a tremendous advantage over a well-educated white in terms of the job market. I think sometimes a black may think they don't have an advantage or this and that . . . I've said on one occasion, even about myself, if I were starting off today, I would love to be a well-educated black, because I believe they do have an actual advantage.

NBC News Special, 1989.

"

"

Black guys counting my money! I hate it. The only kind of people I want counting my money are little short guys that wear yarmulkes every day.

From his 1991 book, Trumped.

"

"

I have a great relationship with the blacks.

From interview at Albany's Talk1300 radio station, April 14, 2011.

"

ON HIMSELF

"

"Sorry losers and haters, but my I.Q. is one of the highest -and you all know it! Please don't feel so stupid or insecure,it's not your fault"

Twitter, May 9, 2013

"

"

I'm a bit of a P.T. Barnum. I make stars out of everyone.

The London Observer, *1991*.

"

"

Money was never a big motivation for me, except as a way to keep score. The real excitement is playing the game.

Twitter, September 13, 2014.

"

"

I actually don't have a bad hairline.

Rolling Stone *interview, 2011*

"

"

I like thinking big. If you're going to be thinking anything, you might as well think big.

Trump: The Art of the Deal, *1987.*

"

"

I have an attention span that's as long as it has to be.

TIME Magazine, *August 18, 2015*

"

"

It is very hard for them to attack me because I am so good looking.

Meet the Press, *August 9, 2015.*

"

"

I have a great temperament. My temperament is very good, very calm.

December 7, 2015.

"

"

"I've never gambled in my life. To me, a gambler is someone who plays slot machines. I prefer to own slot machines. It's a very good business being the house."

Donald J. Trump, Trump: The Art of the Deal

"

"

I just won the Golf Club Championship, probably my last, at Trump International Golf Club, in Palm Beach County, Florida. Such a great honor!

Truth Social post, March 16, 2025

"

"

You're ridiculous … that number's ridiculous; you're way off.

In response to Forbes *estimated the value of the Trump brand at $200 million in 2011. Trump disputed this number saying it was ridiculous and claiming his brand was worth $3 billion.*

"

"

We have a 98 percent approval rating. We have an 'A' from the Better Business Bureau and people like it.

Discussing Trump University, GOP debate, February, 2016.

"

TRUMP TRIVIA

Trump was called 'The Donald' by media outlets who picked up the title from hearing Trump's first wife, Czech-born Ivanka, say his name in broken English. His close friends call him DJT (Donald John Trump).

TRUMP TRIVIA

Trump has been married three times. The first to Ivanka Zelníčková (m. 1977–1991); the second to actress Marla Maples (m. 1993–99); and the third to his current wife, former model Melania Knauss (m. 2005).

"

When you start studying yourself too deeply, you start seeing things that maybe you don't want to see … and if there's a rhyme and a reason. People can figure you out, and once they can figure you out, you're in big trouble.

New York Times, *September 8, 2015.*

"

"

I'm speaking with myself, number one, because I have a very good brain and I've said a lot of things … my primary consultant is myself and I have a very good instinct for this stuff.

Trump shares the name of the person he consults on foreign policy, March 29, 2016.

"

> Well, it's a private little water company, and I supply the water for all my places. And it's good, but it's very good.

On his defunct water company, which was known to have displayed water from a Connecticut bottler who specialises in personalised labels on bulk orders, press conference, 2016.

> Show me someone without an ego, and I'll show you a loser – having a healthy ego, or high opinion of yourself, is a real positive in life!

Facebook, December 10, 2013

> I don't settle lawsuits – very rare – because once you settle lawsuits, everybody sues you – very simple.

On his approach to lawsuits, Trump press conference, 2016.

"

I went to the Wharton School of Finance, I was a great student. ... I go out, I make a tremendous fortune. I write a book called *The Art of the Deal*, the No. 1 selling business book of all time, at least I think, but I'm pretty sure it is. And certainly a big monster, the No. 1 bestseller.

Speaking about his best-selling book, The Art of the Deal, *to Don Lemon on CNN, July 1, 2015. According to politico.com,* Trump: The Art of the Deal *sold one million copies; Stephen Covey's* The 7 Habits of Highly Effective People *sold more than 25 million.*

"

"

I have very successful companies ... I'm going to do this in about two seconds, but let me explain. We have Trump Steaks, and by the way, you want to take one, we'll charge you about – what? – 50 bucks a steak. No, I won't.

twitchy.com, 2016.

"

"

A great friend of mine was a founder of Grey Goose [vodka] and what we're going to do is to top it. I want to top them just because it's fun to top my friends.

On Larry King Live, *1999.*
Trump Vodka was introduced to the market on 2006, it folded as a brand two years later is no longer on sale.

"

"

Islamic terrorism (ISIS) is eating up large portions of the Middle East. They've become rich. I'm in competition with them. They just built a hotel in Syria. Can you believe this? They built a hotel.

On allegations that ISIS built a hotel in Syria, that have been proven to be false. Announcement Speech, June 2015.

"

> I think I'm the most honest human being perhaps that God ever created. Perhaps.

Rally in Selma, North Carolina, April 12, 2022.

> I do love provoking people. There is truth to that. I love competition, and sometimes competition is provoking people. I don't mind provoking people. Especially when they're the right kind of people.

Buzzfeed, 2014.

ON BEING RICH AND FAMOUS

"

I think apologizing is a great thing, but you have to be wrong. I will absolutely apologize, sometime in the hopefully distant future, if I'm ever wrong.

Speaking on The Tonight Show *with Jimmy Fallon, 2015.*

"

"

"One of the problems when you become successful is that jealousy and envy inevitably follow. There are people – I categorize them as life's losers – who get their sense of accomplishment and achievement from trying to stop others. As far as I'm concerned, if they had any real ability they wouldn't be fighting me, they'd be doing something constructive themselves."

Donald J. Trump, Trump: The Art of the Deal

"

"

I've already got my own airplane. We could save money on Air Force One.

On his intention to run for president, 'Liberties; Living la Vida Trumpa' by Maureen Dowd, New York Times, November 17, 1999.

"

"

Owning great landmarks such as the Empire State Building or Trump Tower or the General Motors Building or the Plaza Hotel – there are certain just spectacular landmarks – it's an honor.

BrainyQuote

"

"

The show is 'Trump' and it has sold out performances everywhere. I've had fun doing it and will continue to have fun, and I think most people enjoy it.

Playboy, March 1990.

"

TRUMP TRIVIA

Trump has fathered five children with his three wives. Donald Jr (b.1977), Ivanka (b.1981), Eric (b.1984), Tiffany (b.1993) and Barron (b.2006). Trump also has ten grandchildren.

TRUMP TRIVIA

From *Wrestlemania* to the White House? In 2013, Trump was inducted into the World Wrestling Entertainment Inc. (WWE) Hall of Fame. 'Donald Trump is a *WrestleMania* institution,' Vince McMahon said at The Donald's induction. In 1988, Trump brought in *Wrestlemania IV* for the opening of Trump Plaza in Atlantic City. Trump Plaza closed in 2014. The pair latter battled it out, using proxy wrestlers, in *Wrestlemania XXIII*, with McMahon losing and having to shave his head!

"

I mean, part of the beauty of me is that I'm very rich. So if I need $600 million, I can put $600 million myself. That's a huge advantage. I must tell you, that's a huge advantage over the other candidates.

On the media release of a one page prepared financial disclosure statement, ABC News, 2015.

"

ON IMMIGRATION

"

So when I heard 10,000 and 3,000 a number, you know, from one of you – I'd say all right. But now we're talking about 200,000. Obama is getting carried away again with this whole thing about immigration. And now we hear 200,000 and it could very well be ISIS.

At a campaign stop in Franklin, Tennessee, October 3, 2015.

"

"

You have the migration because Syria is such a disaster. And now I hear we want to take in 200,000 Syrians, right? And they could be, listen, they could be ISIS. I don't know.

Campaign speech, Keene, New Hampshire, September 2015.
The 200,000 figure cited is in fact more than the entire allotment of refugees worldwide that the U.S. hopes to accept over the next two years.

"

"

[I am] calling for a total and complete shutdown of Muslims entering the United States until our country's representatives can figure out what is going on.

Policy statement, December 7, 2015.

"

ON BIRTHRIGHT LAWS

"

And you know, in the case of other countries, including Mexico, they don't do that. It doesn't work that way. You don't walk over the border for one day and all of a sudden we have another American citizen. It doesn't work that way. Mexico doesn't do it. Other places don't do it. Very few places do it. We're the only place, just about, that's stupid enough to do it.

Campaign speech, August 2015.

"

ON MEXICO/LATINOS

"

I will build a great wall – and nobody builds walls better than me, believe me – and I'll build them very inexpensively. I will build a great, great wall on our southern border, and I will make Mexico pay for that wall. Mark my words.

June 16, 2015.

"

> I'm not just saying Mexicans, I'm talking about people from all over that are killers and rapists and they're coming into this country.
>
> *On CNN's State of the Union talk show, June 28, 2015.*

> All I'm doing is telling the truth. Someone's doing the raping, Don. Who's doing the raping? Who's doing the raping?
>
> *To Don Lemon on CNN, July 2, 2015, when questioned about Mexican immigrants being rapists.*

> Our leaders are stupid, our politicians are stupid, and the Mexican government is much sharper.
>
> *GOP debate, August 2015*

"

When Mexico sends its people, they're not sending their best. They're not sending you. They're sending people that have lots of problems, and they're bringing those problems with us. They're bringing drugs. They're bringing crime. They're rapists. And some, I assume, are good people.

Presidential announcement speech, June 2015. Trump later published a statement that stated his comments were 'deliberately distorted by the media'.

"

"

The Mexican government is much smarter, much sharper, much more cunning. And they send the bad ones over because they don't want to pay for them. They don't want to take care of them.

To Fox News *journalist Chris Wallace, August 6, 2015.*

"

"

You're going to have a deportation force, and you're going to do it humanely ... you have millions of people that are waiting in line to come into this country and they're waiting to come in legally. And I always say the wall, we're going to build the wall. It's going to be a real deal. It's going to be a real wall.

On plans to deport 11 million illegal immigrants and their legally US-born children, on MSNBC's Morning Joe show, November 2015.

"

ON THE WORLD TRADE CENTRE ATTACK

"

I watched when the World Trade Center came tumbling down. And I watched in Jersey City, New Jersey, where thousands and thousands of people were cheering as that building was coming down. Thousands of people were cheering.

Rally, Birmingham, Alabama, November 2015.

"

"

Chuck, I saw it on television.
So did many other people.
And many, many people. I said hundreds.

In response to questions of how many people are alleged to have celebrated the 9/11 attack. NBC's Meet the Press *with Chuck Todd, November 2015.*

"

"

The wife knew exactly what was happening. They left two days early, with respect to the World Trade Center, and they went back to where they went, and they watched their husband on television flying into the World Trade Center, flying into the Pentagon.

GOP debate, March 2016.

"

TRUMP TRIVIA

In 2012, during the US presidential campaign, Trump offered to give $5 million to charity if US President Barack Obama would release his birth certificate and college records. He later allegedly upped the offer to $50 million. When asked to supply his college records and birth certificate by various media organizations, Trump declined. US political commentator Bill Maher then offered Trump $5 million dollars if he would produce his birth certificate to prove his father was not 'an orangutan', Trump did so and then sued Maher for the $5 million. The matter did not proceed to court after it was pointed out to Trump that Maher was making 'a joke' and the courts would deem it such.

ON JOBS

"

A lot of people up there can't get jobs. They can't get jobs, because there are no jobs, because China has our jobs and Mexico has our jobs. They all have jobs.

June 16, 2015.
Official statistics showed 5.4 million job openings at the time – the most in 15 years.

"

RUNNING FOR PRESIDENT

"

I could stand in the middle of Fifth Avenue and shoot somebody, and I wouldn't lose any voters.

Sioux Center, Iowa rally, January 23, 2016.

"

"

I don't want to be president. I'm 100 percent sure.
I'd change my mind only if I saw this country continue
to go down the tubes.

Playboy, *March 1990.*

"

"

Look, I'm a negotiator like you folks; we're negotiators …
I know why you're not going to support me. You're not going
to support me because I don't want your money.

*Speaking at the Republican Jewish Coalition,
December 3, 2015.*

"

"

It would be a shame … I will say that people who are
following me are very passionate. They love this country and
they want this country to be great again.'

*On hearing two of his followers beat an Hispanic man,
August 20, 2015.*

"

"

We won with poorly educated. I love the poorly educated.

Donald Trump on his performance with 'poorly educated' voters who helped him win the Nevada Caucus, February 23, 2016.

"

"

Just so you understand, I don't know anything about David Duke, OK? I don't know anything about what you're even talking about with white supremacy or white supremacists. So I don't know. I don't know – did he endorse me, or what's going on? Because I know nothing about David Duke; I know nothing about white supremacists.

Refusing to condemn former Ku Klux Klan grand wizard and noted white supremacist David Duke, who endorsed Trump for president, to CNN's Jake Tapper, February 28, 2016.

"

TRUMP TRIVIA

In 2010 Trump received an honorary degree from Robert Gordon University in Scotland. In 2015, the degree was revoked after Trump made statements that were 'wholly incompatible with the ethos and values of the university.' Scottish First Minister Nicola Sturgeon later stripped Trump of his role as a 'business ambassador' for Scotland.

"

The Reform Party now includes a Klansman, Mr. Duke, a neo-Nazi, Mr. [Patrick] Buchanan, and a communist, Ms. [Lenora] Fulani. This is not company I wish to keep.

Trump, in a statement saying he will not accept the Reform Party nomination for president, February 13, 2000.

"

"

For the most part, you can't respect people because most people aren't worthy of respect.

Never Enough: Donald Trump and the Pursuit of Success, *2015*

"

"

I think you'd have riots. I think you'd have riots. I'm representing many, many millions of people. In many cases first-time voters ... If you disenfranchise those people? And you say, well, I'm sorry, you're 100 votes short, even though the next one is 500 votes short? I think you'd have problems like you've never seen before. I wouldn't lead it, but I think bad things will happen.

On what will happen if the nomination is taken from him at the Republican convention, CNN, 2016.

"

"

I watch the speeches of these people, and they say 'the sun will rise, the moon will set', all sorts of wonderful things will happen, and the people are saying, 'What is going on? I just want a job.'

Campaign speech, June 2015.

"

"

I'm well acquainted with winning …
That's what this country needs now.

Announcing to the Conservative Political Action Conference that he would play a key role in choosing the 2012 GOP Candidate, February 10, 2011.

"

"

I'm not a bad person. I'm just doing my thing – I'm, you know, running. I want to do something that's good. It's not an easy thing to do. I had a nice life until I did this, you know. This is a very difficult thing to do.

Asking for a fair go from the press, Washington Post, *March 21, 2016.*

"

TRUMP TRIVIA

Trump is a Gemini. According to sunsigns.org. people born on 14 June are not normally timid. They will usually speak their mind but are open to rebuttal. They also possess the ability to be astute leaders and can 'throw people off guard with their range of knowledge'. They are risk takers seeking purpose and financial stability; they enjoy discovering and learning and are extremely health conscious. 'The Twins' star sign finds people born on 14 June are intelligent and multifaceted, but they crave adventure, are impulsive and are contrary by nature. People born on this day crave emotional and financial security. They are likely to choose between a career and a family, and though they may not be the perfect parent or husband, they will be a big part of the children's lives.

"

One of the key problems today is that politics is such a disgrace. Good people don't go into government.

The Advocate, 2000.
Trump explored running for US president in 2000 as a candidate for the Reform Party, before announcing his candidacy for the Republican Party in 2015.

"

"

Our country is in serious trouble. We don't have victories anymore. We used to have victories, but we don't have them. When was the last time anybody saw us beating, let's say China, in a trade deal? I beat China all the time. All the time.

From his speech official announcing he would be entering the Republican primary for president, June 16, 2015.

"

"

I will be the greatest jobs president that God ever created. I will bring back our jobs from China, from Mexico, from Japan, from so many places. I'll bring back our jobs and I'll bring back our money.

From his announcement speech, June 16, 2015.

"

"

Out of 67 counties [in Florida], I won 66, which is unprecedented. It's never happened before."

March 21, 2016.
Trump has a short memory. John Kerry (Democrat) and George W. Bush (Republican) won all 67 counties for their respective parties in 2004.

"

"

I have joined the political arena so that the powerful can no longer beat up on people that cannot defend themselves.
Nobody knows the system better than me, which is why I alone can fix it.
I have seen firsthand how the system is rigged against our citizens, just like it was rigged against Bernie Sanders – he never had a chance.

Republican nomination acceptance speech, July 21, 2016.

"

"

Abraham Lincoln was a Republican … people say 'I didn't know that'.

Republican undraising dinner, March 22, 2017. Pew Research Centre survey of Americans in April 2012 found 55 percent knew Lincoln was Republican.

"

> "Despite the constant negative press covfefe"
>
> *Twitter post, 12:06 AM, May 31, 2017*
>
> Who can figure out the true meaning of "covfefe" ??? Enjoy!
>
> *Twitter post, 8:09 PM May 31, 2017*

> "I think the president and a small group of people know exactly what he meant."
>
> *White House Press Secretary Sean Spicer*

"

I hope they arrest these people, because honestly they should be … the only way to stop the craziness is to press charges.

Trump threatens to get tough with protestors at his rallies, Fox News, March 13, 2016.

"

ON CAMPAIGN DONATIONS

"

"For Hillary Clinton, I said be at my wedding and she came to my wedding. She had no choice because I gave to a foundation that frankly that foundation is supposed to do good. I didn't know her money would be used on private jets going all over the world. It was."

GOP debate, Fox News, August 2016

"

> "Most of the people on this stage I've given to, just to you understand, a lot of money."

GOP debate, Fox News, August 2016

> Steve Jobs would not be happy that his wife is wasting money he left her on a failing Radical Left Magazine that is run by a con man (Goldberg) and spews FAKE NEWS & HATE. Call her, write her, let her know how you feel!!!
>
> Twitter, September 5, 2020

Laurene Powell Jobs donated at least $500,000 to Joe Biden's campaign.

AT PRESIDENTIAL RALLIES

"

We will have so much winning if I get elected you may get bored with winning. Believe me. We are going to start winning big league.

Campaign speech, December 2015. Debate began immediately whether Trump said "big league" or "bigly".
It was eventually agreed that he had said "big league". The word "bigly" is now recognised in may dictionaries as meaning 'in a big or impressive way or to a large degree'.

"

"

I love the old days, you know? You know what I hate? There's a guy totally disruptive, throwing punches, we're not allowed punch back anymore… I'd like to punch him in the face, I'll tell ya.

Donald Trump on how he would handle a protester in Nevada, sparking roaring applause from the audience, February 22, 2016.

"

TRUMP TRIVIA

Trump's birthstone is agate, a gemstone that represents 'prosperity, good luck, long life and strength'.

"

There may be somebody with tomatoes in the audience. If you see somebody getting ready to throw a tomato, knock the crap out of them, would you? Seriously. Okay? Just knock the hell – I promise you, I will pay for the legal fees. I promise, I promise.

Cedar Rapids, Iowa, February 1, 2016. Trump later changed his mind after a supporter king hit a black protester in North Carolina.

"

"

'I don't condone violence at all.'

Trump to George Stephanopoulos, March 15, 2016.

"

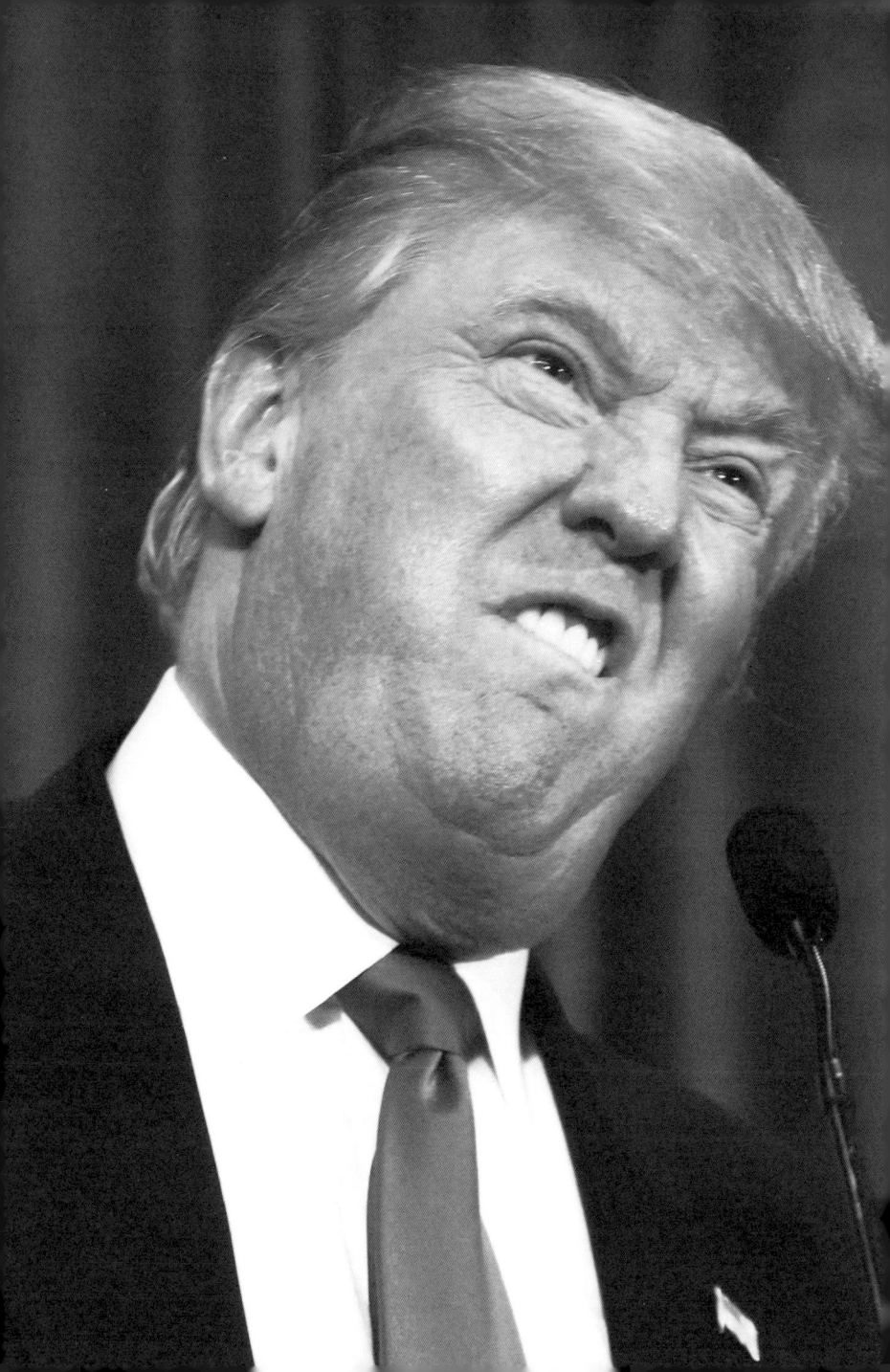

"

Here's a guy, throwing punches, nasty as hell, screaming at everything else, when we're talking … the guards are very gentle with him. He's walking out, like, big high-fives, smiling, laughing … I'd like to punch him in the face, I tell ya.

Las Vegas, February 22, 2016.

"

"

Wouldn't you love to see one of these NFL owners, when somebody disrespects our flag, you'd say, 'Get that son of a bitch off the field right now. Out! He's fired. He's fired!

Speech at a rally in Huntsville, AL referring to protests by NFL players against the U.S. flag, September 2017

"

TRUMP TRIVIA

Trump does not smoke, drink alcohol and has not taken drugs. In *Trump: Surviving at the Top* (1990) he wrote 'I've yet to have my first cup of coffee'.

TRUMP TRIVIA

Trump magazine was a quarterly that folded in 2009. When questioned about its failure, Trump threw a magazine to fans on stage at a March 9, 2016 rally. This was a copy of *The Jewel of Palm Beach*, which is offered to guests at Trump's Mar-a-Lago resort in Florida … not *Trump* magazine.

"

At what point do people blame the protesters. These people are professional agitators … very disruptive people … sick, protestors … I think maybe those people have some blame and should suffer some blame also.

Trump paradoxically blames the protestors for the violence handed out against them at his rallies.
The Guardian, *March 21, 2016.*

"

"

The word "tariff" is the most beautiful word in the dictionary – more beautiful than "love", more beautiful than "respect". No, less beautiful than "religion", no. Right? I don't want to get into that argument. But the word "tariff" is the most beautiful word in the dictionary, remember that. It's going to make our country, it's going to make our country rich, and our politicians were too stupid for so many years or something else was going on.

Campaign Rally in Latrobe, Pennsylvania, October 19, 2024

"

> In Springfield, they are eating the dogs, … they're eating the pets of the people that live there.
>
> *Harris v Trump Presidential debate, September 10, 2024*

AT PRESIDENTIAL DEBATES

> Well, I turned out to be right. Before the end of the debate I gave them [the Fox moderators] the 'A' – we had it sent to us – and here's the 'A' rating from the Better Business Bureau, and they refused to put it on that night … So we have an 'A' rating not a 'D minus' rating.
>
> *Detroit debate, March, 2016.*

"

I can be more presidential than anybody ... When I have 16 people coming at me from 16 different angles, you don't want to be so presidential. You have to win; you have to beat them back. I would be more presidential ... than anybody but the great Abe Lincoln. He was very presidential. Right?

Primaries election night speech, March 8, 2016.

"

"

I'm self-funding my campaign. Nobody is going to be taking care of me. I don't want anybody's money.

Speaking at the 10th GOP debate in Miami, March 11, 2016.

"

"

We're way ahead of everybody. I don't think you can say that we don't get it automatically … I think you'd have riots. I'm representing many, many millions of people … I think you would see problems like you've never seen before. I think bad things would happen. I really do.

Trump warning his own party on CNN what might happen if he was denied the party's presidential nomination, March 16, 2016.

"

"

I think whoever gets to the top position as opposed to solving that artificial number that was by somebody, which is a very random number, I think that whoever gets the most delegates should win.

Complaining that he may not obtain an 'absolute majority' of votes to secure the GOP nomination, March 11, 2016. Rather than being a 'random number' 1,237 votes is actually a simple majority of the 2,472 delegate votes.

"

"

We're not allowed to fight. We can't fight. We're not knocking out the oil because they don't want to create environmental pollution up in the air. I mean, these are things that nobody even believes. They think we're kidding. They didn't want to knock out the oil because of what it's going to do to the carbon footprint.

On climate change (sort of) at the CNN GOP debate, March 10, 2016.
The US stepped up attacks on oil facilities controlled by the Islamic State when it launched "Operation Tidal Wave II" on October 21, 2015, but the administration expressed concern that unilateral air strikes against oil and natural gas facilities will cause long-term economic and local environmental damage that could hurt Syria's post-war recovery.

"

"

They're a very dishonest lot, generally speaking, in the world of politics.

During the Fox News *debate, August 2015.*

"

TRUMP TRIVIA

Over the years Trump has used his name to sell casinos, resorts, condominiums, 'university' courses, an airline, a mortgage company, reality TV shows, steaks, vodka, wine, spring water, chocolate bars, clothing, board games, video games and various merchandising.

TRUMP TRIVIA

Trump Winery is a registered trade name of Eric Trump Wine Manufacturing LLC, which is not owned, managed, or affiliated with Donald J Trump, the Trump Organization or any of their affiliates.

"

MEGYN KELLY: "Mr. Trump, one of the things people love about you is you speak your mind and you don't use a politician's filter. However, that is not without its downsides, in particular, when it comes to women. You've called women you don't like 'fat pigs, dogs, slobs, and disgusting animals.'"

TRUMP: "Only Rosie O'Donnell."

GOP debate, Fox News, August 2016

"

"

Education through Washington, D.C., I don't want that. I want local education. I want the parents, and I want all of the teachers, and I want everybody to get together around a school and to make education great.

Speaking during a primary debate in Miami, March 10, 2016.

"

BEING PRESIDENT

"

I looked out, the field was, looked like million, million and a half people. They showed a field where there was practically nobody standing there. And they said, "Donald Trump did not draw well." I said, "It was almost raining!" The rain should've scared them away but God looked down and said we're not going to let it rain on your speech.

Speaking at the CIA Headquarters about his inauguration crowd and the press coverage, FOX 10 Phoenix, 21 January 2017

"

"

1.3 million people from ages 150 to 159. And over 130,000 people, according to the Social Security databases, are aged over 160 years old. We have a healthier country than I thought, Bobby.

Address to joint session of Congress, 4 March 2025

"

"

Now that Russian collusion after one year of intense study has proven to be a total hoax on the American public the Democrats and their lapdogs the Fake News Mainstream Media are taking out the old Ronald Reagan playbook and screaming mental stability and intelligence..... ....Actually, throughout my life, my two greatest assets have been mental stability and being, like, really smart. Crooked Hillary Clinton also played these cards very hard and, as everyone knows, went down in flames. I went from VERY successful businessman, to top T.V. Star..... ....to President of the United States (on my first try). I think that would qualify as not smart, but genius....and a very stable genius at that!

Twitter, January 6 2018

"

"

Like in 2017, we will again build the strongest military the world has ever seen. We will measure our success not only by the battles we win but also by the wars that we end – and perhaps most importantly, the wars we never get into.

Inaugural address, January 20, 2025

"

"

This week, I will also end the government policy of trying to socially engineer race and gender into every aspect of public and private life. We will forge a society that is colorblind and merit-based. As of today, it will henceforth be the official policy of the United States government that there are only two genders: male and female.

Inaugural address, January 20, 2025

"

"

And now we're going to go and drill, baby, drill, and do all the things that we've wanted to do and bring your costs down, your prices down, and make our country safe.

Document Signing Ceremony following the Inaugural Parade at Capitol One Arena, January 20, 2025

"

Trump's mug shot released by the Fulton County, Georgia sheriff's office, August 24, 2023.

Opposite: Official presidential portrait, 2024.

"

Just a few months ago, in a beautiful Pennsylvania field, an assassin's bullet ripped through my ear. But I felt then and believe even more so now that my life was saved for a reason. I was saved by God to Make America Great Again.

20 Jan 2025 Inaugural address

"

"

The bottom line is, the percentage of Americans who say we're on the right track is through the roof.

Truth Social post, March 26, 2025

"

"

I build beautiful ballrooms … like I have at Mar-a-Lago, as beautiful as it can be.

Trump talking about an addition to the White House, New York Post, *April 13, 2025*

"

"

It was a pleasure to have dinner the other night with Governor Justin Trudeau of the Great State of Canada. I look forward to seeing the Governor again soon so that we may continue our in depth talks on Tariffs and Trade, the results of which will be truly spectacular for all! DJT

Truth Social post, December 10, 2024

"

ON THE ECONOMY

"

The last quarter, it was just announced, our gross domestic product … was below zero. Who ever heard of this? It's never below zero.

Quoted in an article by Louis Jacobson,
politifact.com, June 16, 2015.
In the US, economic growth has been below zero
42 times since 1946.

"

"

GDP was zero essentially for the last two quarters. If that ever happened in China you would have had a depression like nobody's ever seen before. They go down to 7 percent, 8 percent, and it's a – it's a national tragedy. We're at zero, we're not doing anything.

March 11, 2016. Real GDP grew at a rate of 2 percent in the third quarter of 2015 and 1 percent in the fourth quarter according to the February 2016 release from the US Bureau of Economic Analysis.

"

"

The problem in Venezuela is not that socialism has been poorly implemented. It's that socialism has been faithfully implemented.

First address to the United Nations, September 19, 2017.

"

ON BARACK OBAMA

"

I have people that have been studying [Obama's birth certificate] and they cannot believe what they're finding … I would like to have him show his birth certificate, and can I be honest with you, I hope he can. Because if he can't, if he can't, if he wasn't born in this country, which is a real possibility, then he has pulled one of the great cons in the history of politics.

On viewing President Barack Obama's US birth certificate. Today Show, 2011.

"

"

Sadly, because President Obama has done such a poor job as president, you won't see another black president for generations!

ABC News, 2014.

"

"

An 'extremely credible source' has called my office and told me that Barack Obama's birth certificate is a fraud.

Twitter, August 6, 2012.

"

"

There is something on that birth certificate – maybe religion, maybe it says he's a Muslim, I don't know. Maybe he doesn't want that. Or, he may not have one.

Discussing President Barack Obama's birth certificate, The Laura Ingraham Show, *2011.*

"

"

Our weak President, that kisses everybody's arse, is in more wars than I have ever seen. Now he's in Libya, he's in Afghanistan, he's in Iraq. Nobody respects us.'

Speaking on the Bill O'Reilly on Fox show, 2011.

"

"

We are going to be looking at a lot of different things and, you know, a lot of people are saying that.

In response to an audience member who said that President Obama is a Muslim, "not even an American." Town Hall event, Rochester, New Hampshire, 2015.

"

"

So I've been doing deals for a long time. I've been making lots of wonderful deals, great deals. That's what I do. Never, ever, ever in my life have I seen any transaction so incompetently negotiated as our deal with Iran. And I mean never.

Campaign speech, September 2015.

"

TRUMP TRIVIA

Trump has authored and co-authored at least 18 books, including: *Trump: The Art of the Deal* (1987); *Trump: Surviving at the Top* (1990); *Trump: The Art of the Comeback* (1997); *Trump: How to Get Rich* (2004); *Think Big and Kick Ass in Business and Life* (2009); and *Crippled America: How to Make America Great Again* (2015). His Amazon blurb reads … 'DONALD J. TRUMP is the world's most famous businessman, a many-time bestselling author, a political commentator, and owner and host of the hit NBC TV shows *The Apprentice* and *Celebrity Apprentice*'.

TRUMP TRIVIA

Trump, in 2007, was honored by receiving the 2,327th Star on the Hollywood Walk of Fame. Trump's star was for his role on NBC's *The Apprentice*. He was accompanied at the star's unveiling by his wife, Melania Knauss-Trump, and their son Barron. It is situated at 6801 Hollywood Boulevard. In January 2016 the star was defaced by a spray-painted swastika, which was quickly removed by the Hollywood Chamber of Commerce.

"

He grew up and nobody knew him. You know? When you interview people, if ever I got the nomination, if I ever decide to run, you may go back and interview people from my kindergarten. They'll remember me. Nobody ever comes forward. Nobody knows who he is until later in his life. It's very strange. The whole thing is very strange.

Good Morning America, *March 2015.*

"

"

We have a disaster called 'the big lie': Obamacare … And it's going to get worse, because remember, [when] Obamacare really kicks in in 2016. Obama is going to be out playing golf.

Campaign speech, June 2015.

"

"

Our great African American President hasn't exactly had a positive impact on the thugs who are so happily and openly destroying Baltimore!

In response to the violent eruptions in Baltimore after the death of Freddie Gray in police custody. Twitter, April 28, 2015.

"

"

This election is a total sham and a travesty. We are not a democracy!

Twitter, November 7, 2012 after President Obama won the a second term by a margin of almost 4% of the vote.

"

"

If Obama resigns from office NOW, thereby doing a great service to the country – I will give him free lifetime golf at any one of my courses!

Twitter, September 11, 2014.

"

"

Obama is, without question, the WORST EVER president. I predict he will now do something really bad and totally stupid to show manhood!

Twitter, June 6, 2014.

"

"

Every time you walk down the street people are screaming, 'You're fired!'

New York Post, *March 19, 2004.*

"

ON HILARY CLINTON

"

She got schlonged … she lost, I mean she lost.

On Hillary Clinton, December 21, 2015.

"

TRUMP TRIVIA

Trump has a profile on imdb.com (International Movie Database) having made appearances in several movies (*Home Alone 2: Lost in New York*, 1992; *54*, 1998; Woody Allen's *Celebrity*, 1998 and *Zoolander*, 2001) as himself, but he has also graced the small screen on *The Jeffersons* (1985), *The Nanny* (1996), *Spin City* (1998) and *Sex in the City* (1999). Although it's fair to say he will never be nominated for an Oscar with such a narrow dramatic range, he was nominated for back-to-back Primetime Emmy Awards for Outstanding Reality-Competition Program (2004–2005) for *The Apprentice*.

"

I beat Hillary, and I will give you the list. I beat Hillary in many of the polls that have been taken.

*March 17, 2016.
At the time Clinton led Trump in five of the six most recent polls listed. factcheck.org also reports Trump has been ahead in only five out of 49 polls conducted on a hypothetical US presidential match-up since last May.*

"

"

We have Hillary Clinton who wants to destroy and take your guns away. She wants to take your guns away. And frankly you can't do that with an executive order.

January 9, 2016.

"

TRUMP TRIVIA

Trump said he earned more than $213 million over the course of 13 years as the face of the NBC show *The Apprentice* and *Celebrity Apprentice*. That makes more than $15 million a season. NBC later described the claims as 'a complete, total lie' on the *Morning Joe* program, July 16, 2015. Producer Lawrence O'Donnell called Trump 'a hired hand' who made less than a million dollars in his first year and that the program only had 'two good years' in its 13-year run. *The Apprentice* was cancelled in 2015. "You're fired!"

TRUMP TRIVIA

According to TV ratings figures, Trump's *The Apprentice* was a top 10 rating show in its first year on air (2003–04), attracting an average of 20 million viewers. By its 10th season (2010–11) it was rated 113th and attracting a little under 5 million viewers. The seven seasons of *Celebrity Apprentice* regularly attracted audiences of between 7 and 11 million but made the top 50 shows only once, in its debut season (2007–08). That's show business!

"

If Hilary Clinton can't satisfy her husband,
what makes her think she can satisfy America?

*Twitter, April 16, 2015 with Trump's handle
(@realDonaldTrump) on it. Trump later stated it was
a staffer who retweeted this.*

"

"

I really haven't gone after Hillary yet and there's a lot to go after.

Trump fires an ominous warning to Fox News,
December 23, 2015.

"

"

The Hillary Clinton staged event yesterday was pathetic. Be careful Hillary as you play the war on women or women being degraded card.

*Trump earlier warns Hillary Clinton about being 'sexist'
in the campaign, Twitter, December 24, 2015.*

"

"

Hillary, when you complain about "a penchant for sexism," who are you referring to. I have great respect for women.
BE CAREFUL!

Trumps repeats the warning, Twitter, December 24, 2015.

"

"

Don't believe the @FoxNews Polls, they are just another phony hit job on me. I will beat Hillary Clinton easily in the General Election.

Twitter, March 27, 2016. At the time all major polls, not only Fox, had Clinton leading the hypothetical presidential face-off by more than 4% points.

"

"

The disdain that Hillary Clinton expressed for millions of decent Americans disqualifies her from public service. You cannot run for president if you have such contempt in your heart for the American voter, and she does. You can't lead this nation if you have such a low opinion of its citizens.

National Guard Association conference in Baltimore, September 2016, responding to Hillary Clinton's recent speech in New York stating "You know, to just be grossly generalistic, you could put half of Trump's supporters into what I call the basket of deplorables. Right? They're racist, sexist, homophobic, xenophobic, Islamophobic – you name it"

"

ON JOE BIDEN

"

Sleepy Joe has been in politics for 40 years, and did nothing. Now he pretends to have the answers. He doesn't even know the questions.

Twitter, June 3, 2020

"

"

He's shaking hands with the air. He's walking around – somewhat bewildered – I'd say it's no good – and taking orders from the Easter Bunny."

Rally in Ohio, April 23, 2022

"

"

I was actually sticking up for Sleepy Joe Biden while on foreign soil. Kim Jong Un called him a "low IQ idiot," and many other things, whereas I related the quote of Chairman Kim as a much softer "low IQ individual." Who could possibly be upset with that?

Twitter, May 29, 2019

"

"

So pathetic to see Sleepy Joe Biden, who with his son, Hunter, and to the detriment of the American Taxpayer, has ripped off at least two countries for millions of dollars, calling for my impeachment - and I did nothing wrong. Joe's Failing Campaign gave him no other choice!

Tweet October 10, 2019, following impeachment proceedings Trump over a July phone call he had with Ukrainian President Volodymyr Zelenskiy asking him to investigate Biden and his son Hunter.

"

"

Well, he's right. He did beat Medicare; he beat it to death.

Trump–Biden presidential debate, June 27, 2024

"

ON KAMALA HARRIS

"

Campaigning could take a toll on a family and family life. Although I hear that Kamala and her husband carve out some really beautiful alone time at the end of the day for an intimate dinner. Just Doug, her and the teleprompter that she uses quite well.

Remarks at the Alfred E. Smith Memorial Foundation Dinner in New York City, October 17, 2024

"

Who is negotiating for us in the Middle East? Bombs are dropping all over the place! Sleepy Joe is sleeping on a Beach in California, viciously Exiled by the Democrats, and Comrade Kamala is doing a campaign bus tour with Tampon Tim, her really bad V.P. Pick. Let's not have World War III, because that's where we're heading!

Truth Social post, August 26, 2024

"

> Lyin' Kamala Harris, the Biden appointed "Border Czar" who never visited the Border, and whose incompetence gave us the WORST and MOST DANGEROUS Border anywhere in the World, has absolutely terrible pole numbers against a fine and brilliant young man named DONALD J. TRUMP! Be careful what you wish for, Democrats??? MAGA2024
>
> *Truth Social post, July 22, 2024*

> Is she Indian or is she Black? I respect either one, but she obviously doesn't, because she was Indian all the way and then all of a sudden, she made a turn and she went, she became a Black person.
>
> *Questioned at the National Association of Black Journalists conference in Chicago, July 31, 2024.*

ON REPUBLICAN RIVALS

"

Some of the candidates, they went in, they didn't know the air conditioner didn't work. They sweated like dogs. They didn't know the room was too big because they didn't have anybody there. How are they going to beat ISIS?

On his GOP rivals, June 16, 2015.

"

"

He's a war hero because he was captured. I like people who weren't captured. Perhaps he's a war hero.

On Sen. John McCain for his years-long captivity during the Vietnam War, July 18, 2015.

"

"

Lyin' Ted Cruz just used a picture of Melania from a G.Q. shoot in his ad. Be careful, Lyin' Ted, or I will spill the beans on your wife!

Twitter, March 23, 2016 after someone posted a sexy image of Melania Trump – first used on a 2000 GQ article when the model was Trump's girlfriend – with the heading 'Meet Melania Trump. Your new first lady. Or, you could support Ted Cruz on Tuesday.'

"

"

That's why we call him Lyin' Ted!

Trump rejects Ted Cruz' claim that the photo of Trump's wife did not come from his campaign camp, March 24, 2016.

"

"

He's a desperate person. He's a sad and he's a pathetic person. … He doesn't even use his last name in his ads. He's a sad person who has gone absolutely crazy. I mean, this guy is a nervous wreck. I've never seen anything like it.

Speaking about Jeb Bush, Republican opponent and former Governor of Florida on CNN, February, 2016.

"

"

How stupid are the people of Iowa – How stupid are the people the country – to believe this crap?

In reference to claims made by GOP rival Ben Carson, November 13, 2015.

"

"

Marco Rubio is a total lightweight who I wouldn't hire to run one of my smaller companies - a highly overrated politician!

Twitter, 10 Nov 2015. President-elect Trump chose Marco Rubio as secretary of state in November, 2024

"

"

A disgruntled boring fool who only wanted to go to war. Never had a clue, was ostracized & happily dumped. What a dope!

Responding to John Bolton's book, Twitter, June 18, 2020

"

ON TERROR AND TERRORISM

"

I wrote a very political book years ago in the year 2000, *The America We Deserve*, and I said in that book that we better be careful with this guy named Osama bin Laden. I mean I really study this stuff … Nobody really knew who he was. But he was nasty. He was saying really nasty things about our country and what he wants to do to it. And I wrote in the book [in] 2000 – two years before the World Trade Center came down – I talked to you about Osama bin Laden, you better take him out. I said he's going to crawl under a rock. You better take him out. And now people are seeing that, they're saying, "You know, Trump predicted Osama bin Laden" – which actually is true. And two years later, a year and a half later he knocked down the World Trade Center.

Interview on the Alex Jones Radio Show, *December 2, 2015. The America We Deserve, which was published in January 2000, makes a single reference to bin Laden but it doesn't warn to 'take him out'.*

"

"

I'm the only one on this stage that said: 'Do not go into Iraq. Do not attack Iraq.' Nobody else on this stage said that. And I said it loud and strong.

February 14, 2016.

"

"

Just announced that as many as 5,000 ISIS fighters have infiltrated Europe. Also, many in U.S. I TOLD YOU SO! I alone can fix this problem!

Twitter, March 24, 2016.

"

"

Europe and the U.S. must immediately stop taking in people from Syria. This will be the destruction of civilization as we know it! So sad!

Twitter, March 24, 2016.

"

TRUMP TRIVIA

Air traffic in Palm Beach, Spanish broadcaster Univision, chefs José Andrés and Geoffrey Zakaran, the town of Ossining (New York), Rancho Palos Verdes (California), his publisher, Miss USA contestant Sheena Monnin, comedian Bill Maher, Deutsche Bank, business partner Richard T. Fields, the 'Queen of Mean' Leona Helmsley, … what do they have in common? They were all sued (or threatened to be sued) by Donald Trump (the atlantic.com, March 20, 2013).

"

If they could expand the laws, I would do a lot more than waterboarding … You have to get the information from these people. And we have to be smart. And we have to be tough. We can't be soft and weak.

How Trump would handle terrorist interrogations in wake of the Brussels attacks, NBC interview, March 22, 2016.

"

"

I dealt with Qaddafi. I rented him a piece of land. He paid me more for one night than the land was worth for two years, and then I didn't let him use the land. That's what we should be doing. I don't want to use the word 'screwed', but I screwed him. That's what we should be doing.

Phone interview with Fox and Friends, March 2011.

"

"

I'm the worst thing that's ever happened to ISIS.

To Barbara Walters, in answer to a concern that he is playing into the terrorists' hands, December 8, 2015.

"

ON VLADIMIR PUTIN

"

Putin said very nice things about me. And I say very nicely, wouldn't it be nice if actually we could get along with Russia, we could get along with foreign countries, instead of spending trillions and trillions of dollars? It is always a great honor to be so nicely complimented by a man so highly respected within his own country and beyond.

December 15, 2015.

"

"

[Putin] is a strong leader ...
he's making mincemeat of our president.

December 20, 2015.

"

"

I got to know [Putin] very well because we were both on *60 Minutes* ... we were stablemates, and we did very well that night.

November 10, 2015.
The two did appear on the same 60 Minutes *episode on September 27, 2015, but Putin was interviewed in Moscow and Trump in New York.*

"

"

There are a lot of killers. We've got a lot of killers.
What do you think – our country's so innocent?
You think our country's so innocent?
… take a look at what we've done too. We made
a lot of mistakes. … a lot of people were killed.
A lot of killers around, believe me.

Interview on The O'Reilly Factor after Bill O'Reilly states "Putin's a killer", February 6, 2017.

"

"

I want everybody to stop dying! They're dying!
Russians and Ukrainians – I want them to stop dying.

CNN Republican Presidential Town Hall when asked if he wants Russians or Ukranians to win the war, May 11, 2023

"

ON CHINA

"

The problem with our country is we don't manufacture anything anymore. The stuff that's been sent over from China falls apart after a year and a half. It's crap.

Speaking on Fox News, *2010.*
David Letterman later exposed Trump's clothing range as being made in China, Mexico and Bangladesh when Trump was on his show in October 2012.

"

"

I've read hundreds of books about China over the decades. I know the Chinese. I've made a lot of money with the Chinese. I understand the Chinese mind.

May 4, 2011

"

"

We have a $505 billion trade deficit [with China] right now.

September 16, 2015.
The trade deficit with China for 2015 was $366 billion, according to official Census Bureau figures. Trump's '$505 billion' figure is closer to the US's $532 billion net trade deficit with all countries in 2015.

"

"

Don't forget China's great, and Xi is a great gentleman. He's now president for life. President for life. And he's great. And look, he was able to do that. I think it's great. Maybe we'll have to give that a shot someday.

Fundraiser, Mar-a-Lago, March, 2018

"

"

Merry Christmas to all, including to the wonderful soldiers of China, who are lovingly, but illegally, operating the Panama Canal.

Truth Social post, December 25, 2024

"

ON NORTH KOREA

"

Frankly, the case could be made to let [Japan] protect themselves against North Korea, they'd probably wipe them out pretty quick.

Wisconsin, March 29, 2016.
Trump added, "We're better off, frankly, if
South Korea is going to protect itself."

"

"

It would be a terrible thing but if they do, they do. Good luck … enjoy yourself, folks.

On the possibility that Japan and North Korea might go to war, March 29, 2016.

"

ON WAR

"

I'm not going to use nuclear, but I'm not going to take it off the table.

When asked by MSNBC's Chris Matthews whether he would state on the record that he would never use nuclear weapons in Europe or the Middle East, March 29, 2016.

"

ON MANUFACTURING

"

I'm going to renegotiate our trade deals. I'm going to bring our jobs back. I'm going to bring our manufacturing back.

Speaking at a town hall event that aired on NBC's Today *show, October 25, 2015.*

"

"

Word is that Ford Motor, because of my constant badgering at packed events, is going to cancel their deal to go to Mexico and stay in U.S.

Twitter, October 26, 2015.

"

TRUMP TRIVIA

A day after a black protestor was attacked at a Donald Trump rally in Alabama on November 21, 2015, the Trump camp retweeted a graph stating the following US murder statistics:

USA Crime Statistics—2015

Blacks killed by whites	2%
Blacks killed by police	1%
Whites killed by police	3%
Whites killed by whites	16%
Whites killed by blacks	81%
Blacks killed by blacks	97%

Crime Statistics Bureau—San Francisco

The first problem is that 2015 was not finished and crime stats were not complete. The second is there is no such Crime Statistics Bureau in San Francisco. Lastly, according to politifact.com, every stat is wrong; most telling the FBI's 2014 stats shows whites killed by whites is actually 82% (5.4 times more than 16%) and whites killed by blacks is only 15% (5.4 times less than the figure quoted). The origin of the graphic was later traced back to English football hooligans in the UK. 'Am I gonna check every statistic?" Trump told Bill O'Reilly on *Fox News* when questioned about the graph's inaccuracy. "All it was is a retweet. It wasn't from me … it came out of a radio show and other places."

"

Do you think I will get credit for keeping Ford in U.S. Who cares, my supporters know the truth. Think what can be done as president!

Twitter, October 25, 2016.
Ford announced a $168 million investment to shift production of 2016 Ford F-650 and F-750 trucks from Mexico to Avon Lake, Ohio, back in March 2014 ... a full year before Trump announced his presidency. Ford will still invest $2.8 billion in Mexican manufacturing plants.

"

"

Don't believe the inclusion [argument from NBC]. They've got Rev. Al Sharpton working for them. He's a con man. You have to understand, Rev. Al is a con man. You know, he tells people, 'I'm going to picket you if you don't give.' This guy's a con man. But I've known him for 20 years. You've got to understand who you're dealing with.

August 5, 2015. Sharpton later called Trump 'the white Don King' [famous African American boxing promoter pal of Sharpton]

"

ON THE MIDDLE EAST

"

Before our eyes a new generation of leaders is transcending the ancient conflicts of tired divisions of the past and forging a future where the Middle East is defined by commerce, not chaos, where it exports technology, not terrorism, and where people of different nations, religions, and creeds are building cities together, not bombing each other out of existence.

… this great transformation has not come from Western interventionalists or flying people in beautiful planes giving you lectures on how to live and how to govern your own affairs. …

In the end the so-called nation-builders wrecked far more nations than they built, and the interventionalists were intervening in complex societies that they did not even understand themselves. They told you how to do it, but they had no idea how to do it themselves.

Peace, prosperity and progress ultimately came not from a radical rejection of your heritage, but rather from embracing your national traditions and embracing that same heritage that you love so dearly, and it's something only you could do.

Speech at the Saudi–US Investment Forum, May 13, 2025.

"

"

We have places in London and other places that are so radicalized that the police are afraid for their own lives.

MSNBC interview, December 8, 2015. London Metropolitan police later rejected the claim and more than 500,000 people signed a petition to ban Trump from entering the UK.

"

"

Nobody wants to say this and nobody wants to shut down religious institutions or anything, but you know, you understand it. A lot of people understand it. We're going to have no choice.

Justifying his plans to close mosques to Sean Hannity on Fox News, *November 11, 2015.*

"

TRUMP TRIVIA

How hard is it? Trump won two primaries in his aborted 2000 presidential campaign after telling voters he would NOT be running as a candidate on the Reform Party ticket.

TRUMP TRIVIA

While Hollywood hasn't rallied around Trump's campaign, celebrities who endorsed the 2016 Presidential candidate include Kid Rock, Dennis Rodman, Mike Tyson, Wayne Newton and Scott Baio (former *Happy Days* star, for those who don't remember who he is).

"

In my speech before over 10,000 people in Myrtle Beach, I merely mimicked what I thought would be a flustered reporter trying to get out of a statement he made long ago.

Trump explaining that he wasn't mocking Serge Kovaleski, Pulitzer Prize-winning journalist, now working for the New York Times, *who has arthrogryposis that limits mobility of joints, November 26, 2015.*

"

"

President Trump declared on Tuesday that the United States should seize control of Gaza and permanently displace the entire Palestinian population of the devastated seaside enclave, … Sounding like the real estate developer he once was, Mr. Trump vowed to turn it into "the Riviera of the Middle East."

The New York Times, *February 5, 2025*

"

> He died like a dog.

Announcing the death of terrorist leader, Abu Bakr al-Baghdadi, October 27, 2019.

> Nice house.

Entering the Al Wajba Palace, Doha, Qatar, May 16, 2025

ON MEDICARE

> We're talking about hundreds of billions of dollars [in savings] if we went out and bid [prescription drug prices] … of course you are.

Speaking at the Fox News GOP debate in Detroit, March 3, 2016. The Washington Post *found the figure was 'nonsense'.*

ON THE ENVIRONMENT

"

It's freezing and snowing in New York--we need global warming!

Twitter, November 8, 2012.

"

"

It's Friday. How many bald eagles did wind turbines kill today? They are an environmental & aesthetic disaster.

Twitter, August 24, 2012.

"

"

So ridiculous. Greta must work on her Anger Management problem, then go to a good old fashioned movie with a friend! Chill Greta, Chill!

Twitter, 12 Dec 2019
Commenting on climate activist Greta Thunberg after she was named Time*'s Person of the Year for 2019.*

"

TRUMP TRIVIA

When former Alaskan governor and failed Vice Presidential candidate Sarah Palin endorsed Trump in January 2016, she described Trump as having "the guts to wear the issues that need to be spoken about and debate on his sleeve, where the rest of some of these establishment candidates, they just wanted to duck and hide. They didn't want to talk about these issues until he brought 'em up. In fact, they've been wearing a political correctness kind of like a suicide vest."

Probably not a good time to mention suicide vests.

"

The concept of global warming was created by and for the Chinese in order to make U.S. manufacturing non-competitive.

Twitter, November 6, 2012.

"

"

NBC News just called it 'The Great Freeze' – coldest weather in years. Is our country still spending money on the GLOBAL WARMING HOAX?"

Twitter, January 25, 2014.

"

"

It's really cold outside, they are calling it a major freeze, weeks ahead of normal. Man, we could use a big fat dose of global warming!

Twitter, October 19, 2015.

"

ON SHORT FINGERS

"

My fingers are long and beautiful as, it has been well documented, are various other parts of my body.

New York Post, 2011, in reference to an article in a satirical magazine that once described him as a 'short-fingered' vulgarian.

"

"

He referred to my hands, if they're small, something else must be small … I guarantee you there's no problem. I guarantee it.

Donald Trump in response to a joke by Republican rival Marco Rubio, GOP presidential debate, March 3, 2016.

"

ON VACCINATIONS

"

No more massive injections. Tiny children are not horses – one vaccine at a time, over time. I am being proven right about massive vaccinations – the doctors lied. Save our children & their future.

Twitter, September 3, 2014.

"

"

I am totally in favor of vaccines. But I want smaller doses over a longer period of time. Same exact amount, but you take this little beautiful baby, and you pump- – I mean, it looks just like it's meant for a horse, not for a child, and we've had so many instances, people that work for me. … [in which] a child, a beautiful child went to have the vaccine, and came back and a week later had a tremendous fever, got very, very sick, now is autistic.

CNN GOP debate, September 17, 2015.

"

MORE QUOTES

"

It's like in golf. A lot of people – I don't want this to sound trivial – but a lot of people are switching to these really long putters, very unattractive. It's weird. You see these great players with these really long putters, because they can't sink three-footers anymore. And, I hate it. I am a traditionalist. I have so many fabulous friends who happen to be gay, but I am a traditionalist.

*Commenting on gay marriage,
May 2011 interview with the* New York Times.

"

"

I have never seen a thin person drinking Diet Coke.

Twitter, October 15, 2012.

"

"

I watched as we built schools in Iraq and they'd be blown up. And we'd build another one and it would get blown up. And we would rebuild it three times. And yet we can't build a school in Brooklyn. We have no money for education, because we can't build in our own country. And at what point do you say hey, we have to take care of ourselves.

Washington Post, March 21, 2016.

"

"

I had one basic big libel suit, it was a very bad system, it was New Jersey. I had a great judge, the first one, and I was going to win it. And then I had another good judge, the second one, and then they kept switching judges. And the third one was a bad judge. That's what happened …

Washington Post, *March 21, 2016.*

"

> Do you mind if I sit back a little bit because your breath is very bad.

To Larry King, Larry King Live, *1989*

> I just left Wayne Gretzky, "The Great One" as he is known in Ice Hockey circles. I said, "Wayne, why don't you run for Prime Minister of Canada, soon to be known as the Governor of Canada – You would win easily, you wouldn't even have to campaign." He had no interest, but I think the people of Canada should start a DRAFT WAYNE GRETZKY Movement. It would be so much fun to watch!

Truth Social post, December 25, 2024

> "Why are we having all these people from shithole countries coming here?"

White House meeting, January 11, 2018 (CNN 2018)

"

@ilduce2016: "It is better to live one day as a lion than 100 years as a sheep."

Quoting fascist Italian dictator Benito Mussolini on Twitter, February 28, 2016.

"

"

We have a country that's in serious trouble. If we're not going to get tough and smart, many, many people are going to get hurt very badly.

Esquire *magazine, February 2016.*

"

"

[The US government] have a 5 billion dollar website. I have so many websites … I hire people. They do a website. It costs me three dollars.

Criticising the HealthCare.gov website, June 18, 2015.

"

"

I heard poorly rated @Morning_Joe speaks badly of me (don't watch anymore). Then how come low I.Q. Crazy Mika, along with Psycho Joe, came..
… to Mar-a-Lago 3 nights in a row around New Year's Eve, and insisted on joining me. She was bleeding badly from a face-lift. I said no!

Twitter, June 29, 2017.

"

> This is an island surrounded by water, big water, ocean water.

Referring to Puerto Rico's Hurricane Maria, September, 2017.

> The kidney has a very special place in the heart.

Speech upon signing of Executive Order on Advancing American Kidney Health, July 10, 2019.

> "I discovered, for the first time but not the last, that politicians don't care too much what things cost. It's not their money."

Donald J. Trump, Trump: The Art of the Deal

"

And then they rigged the election. And then I said, You know what I'll do? I'll run again and I'll shove it up their ass. And that's what I did. So if they would've left us alone, and wouldn't have cheated on the election, and wouldn't have rigged it, I would've been retired right now. I would've been happily doing something else, and instead they have me for four more years.

Speaking at a Kennedy Center dinner, May 19, 2025.

"

"

We're keeping the oil. We have the oil. The oil is secure. We left troops behind only for the oil.

Press conference with Turkish President Recep Tayyip Erdoğan, November 13, 2019.

"

WHO SAID IT?

Answers on page 159.

WHO SAID IT:
DONALD TRUMP OR ELON MUSK?

– 1 –

"We're getting very big in space and we are seriously thinking of the Space Force."

– 2 –

"My family fears that the Russians will assassinate me."

– 3 –

"Past leaders put the United States at the mercy of foreign nations to send our astronauts into orbit — not anymore."

– 4 –

"None of my companies buy advertising or pay famous people to fake endorse."

– 5 –

"Many in America don't realise how proud they should be of the legal system. Not perfect, but nowhere is the cause of justice better served."

– 6 –

"The concept of global warming was created by and for the Chinese in order to make US manufacturing non-competitive."

– 7 –

"The holier-than-thou hypocrisy of big media companies who lay claim to the truth, but publish only enough to sugarcoat the lie, is why the public no longer respects them."

– 8 –

"To be blunt, people would vote for me. They just would. Why? Maybe because I'm so good looking."

– 9 –

"You can tell it's real because it looks so fake."

WHO SAID IT:
DONALD TRUMP OR KAMALA HARRIS

– 10 –

"One must ask, why exactly is it that they don't trust women? Well, we trust women. We trust women."

– 11 –

"Just like our ancestors, w must now come together, rise above past differences, any disagreements have to be put aside and go forward united as one people, one nation ..."

– 12 –

"Fellow Americans, this election is not only the most important of our lives, it is one of the most important in the life of our nation."

– 13 –

"Nothing will sway us, nothing will slow us, and no one will ever stop us. No matter what dangers come our way, no matter what obstacles lie in our path, we will keep striving toward our shared and glorious destiny."

WHO SAID IT: DONALD TRUMP OR JOE BIDEN

– 14 –

"From Phoenix to Flagstaff, from Mesa to Yuma, to the red rocks of Sedona, this great state was settled by some of the toughest men and toughest – and most beautiful – women ever to walk the face of the earth."

– 15 –

"I went to law school on a full academic scholarship, the only one in class that have a full academic scholarship. ... I graduated with three degrees from undergraduate school and 165 credits – I only needed 123 credits. And I'd be delighted to sit down and compare my IQ to yours if you'd like."

– 16 –

"I guess we'll have to compare IQ tests. And I can tell you who is going to win."

– 17 –

"I'm not sorry for anything that I have ever done. I have never been disrespectful intentionally to a man or a woman."

— 18 —

"Nobody has more respect for women than I do. Nobody. Nobody has more respect."

— 19 —

"The press always asks me, 'Don't I wish I were debating him?' No, I wish we were in high school – I could take him behind the gym. That's what I wish."

— 20 —

"What I'm trying to do is go around from town to town. And I'm drawing as big of crowds – bigger than anybody. Have you seen anybody draw bigger crowds than me here in this state?"

— 21 —

"It's packed outside, as you'll be able to see. But it's – they've never seen crowds like this over here."

— 22 —

"You cannot go to a 7-Eleven or a Dunkin' Donuts unless you have a slight Indian accent. I'm not joking."

– 23 –

"I promise you ... you're going to see the single most important thing that changes America. We're gonna cure cancer."

– 24 –

"We will come up with the cures to many, many problems, to many, many diseases – including cancer."

WHO SAID IT: TRUMP OR HILLARY CLINTON?

– 25 –

"So I think we got to have tough conditions tell people to come out of the shadows. If they've committed a crime: deport them. No questions asked. They're gone. If they've been working and a law-abiding, we should say 'Here are the conditions for you to stay: you have to pay a stiff fine because you came here illegally; you have to pay back taxes; and you have to try to learn English; and you have to wait in line.'"

WHO SAID IT:
DONALD TRUMP OR BARACK OBAMA?

– 26 –

"Don't just get involved. Fight for your seat at the table. Better yet, fight for a seat at the head of the table."

– 27 –

"We simply cannot allow people to pour into the United States undetected, undocumented, unchecked, and circumventing the line of people who are waiting patiently, diligently, and lawfully to become immigrants in this country."

– 28 –

"I think I'm running on common sense. I think I'm running on what's right. I don't think in terms of labels."

– 29 –

"So this is not going to be a free ride. It's not going to be some instant amnesty. What's going to happen is you are going to pay a significant fine. You are going to learn English. You are going to go to the back of the line so that you don't get ahead of somebody who was in Mexico City applying legally."

WHO SAID IT: TRUMP OR BERNIE SANDERS?

– 30 –

"If children of 5 are not taught to obey orders, sit still for 7 hours a day, respect their teacher, and raise their hands when they have to go to the bathroom, how will they learn (after 17 more years of education) to become the respectful clerks, technicians and soldiers who keep our society free, our economy strong, and such inspiring men as Richard Nixon and Deane Davis in political office."

– 31 –

"The hedge fund people make a lot of money and they pay very little tax. I want to lower taxes for the middle class.

– 32 –

"In my view, the government of a democratic society has a moral responsibility to play a vital role in making sure all of our people have a decent standard of living."

– 33 –

"The Democratic party has no grassroots."

WHO SAID IT: DONALD TRUMP OR KANYE?

– 34 –

"Also for anyone that has money they know the first rule is to use other people's money."

– 35 –

"We want to innovate and we will win someday."

– 36 –

"My twitter has become so powerful that I can actually make my enemies tell the truth."

– 37 –

"Sorry, there is no STAR on the stage tonight!"

– 38 –

"Entrepreneurs: Be tough, be smart, be personable, but don't take things personally. That's good business."

WHO SAID IT ANSWERS

1. Trump, May 1, 2018
2. Musk
3. Trump, May 30, 2020
4. Musk
5. Musk
6. Trump Tweet, November 7, 2012
7. Musk
8. Trump, *New York Times,* 1999
9. Musk
10. Harris
11. Trump Facebook post, July 20, 2024
12. Harris
13. Trump Facebook post, July 20, 2024
14. Trump, Arizona visit, October 20, 2018
15. Biden, New Hampshire, April 7, 1987
16. Trump, Forbes interview, November 14, 2017
17. Biden, April 5, 2019
18. Trump, Clinton debate, October 20, 2016
19. Biden, Pennsylvania, Oct. 21, 2016
20. Biden, Iowa, August 21, 2019
21. Trump, Indiana, 2018
22. Biden, June 17, 2006
23. Biden, Iowa, June 11, 2019
24. Trump rally, Florida, June 18, 2019
25. Hillary Clinton, February 12, 2008
26. Obama, 2012
27. Obama, news conference, 2005
28. Trump, interview May, 2016
29. Obama, 2005
30. Bernie Sanders
31. Trump, Bloomberg, August 28, 2015
32. Bernie
33. Bernie
34. Kanye
35. Kanye
36. Trump Tweet, October 18, 2012
37. Trump Tweet, October 14, 2015
38. Trump Tweet, June 23, 2015

This Edition published in 2025 by New Holland Publishers

newhollandpublishers.com

Copyright © 2016 New Holland Publishers
Copyright © 2016 in images: New Holland Image Library, Shutterstock or Adobe Stock.

All rights reserved. No part of this publication may be reproduced, stored in a retrieval system or transmitted, in any form or by any means, electronic, mechanical, photocopying, recording or otherwise, without the prior written permission of the publishers and copyright holders.

A record of this book is held at the National Library of Australia.

ISBN 9781760798482

Managing Director: Fiona Schultz
General Manager/Publisher: Olga Dementiev
Designer: Andrew Davies
Production Director: Arlene Gippert
Keep up with New Holland Publishers:
NewHollandPublishers
@newhollandpublishers